self care workbook for teens

BECOMING WHO YOU ARE WITH SELF LOVE & COMPASSION

table of contents

things i can control

FILL IN THE BLANKS!

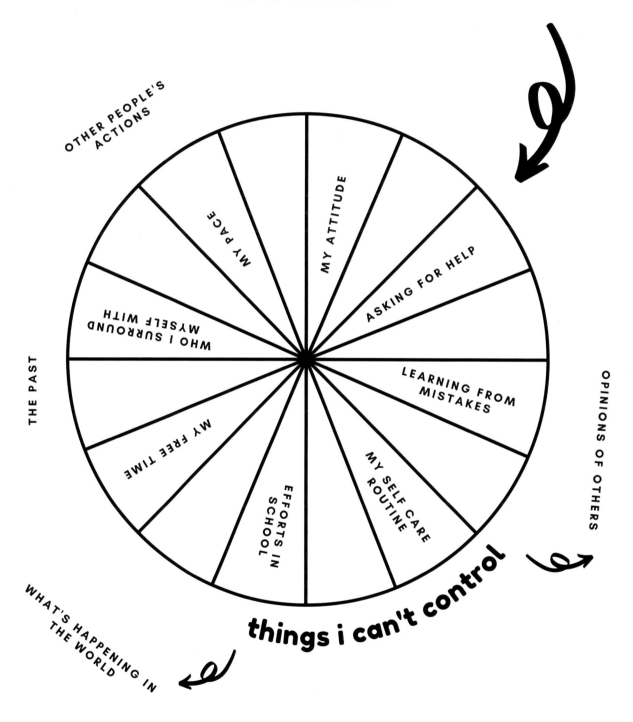

things i can't control

OTHER PEOPLE'S ACTIONS

MY PACE

WHO I SURROUND MYSELF WITH

THE PAST

MY FREE TIME

MY ATTITUDE

ASKING FOR HELP

LEARNING FROM MISTAKES

MY SELF CARE ROUTINE

EFFORTS IN SCHOOL

OPINIONS OF OTHERS

WHAT'S HAPPENING IN THE WORLD

bucket list

BRAINSTORM SOME LIFE GOALS AND ADVENTURES THAT YOU WOULD
LIKE TO TICK OFF - GET INSPIRED!

my self care routine

PLAN OUT YOUR PERFECT DAY FULL OF SELF CARE ACTIVITIES

MORNING ROUTINE

Time & Place

Activity

NIGHT ROUTINE

Time & Place

Activity

----

my future

THINGS TO LOOK FORWARD TO

TRAVEL

SELF GROWTH

FRIENDSHIP

LOVE

CAREER

HOBBIES

ACADEMICS

ADVENTURE

HAPPINESS

visualization

USE THIS PAGE TO VISUALIZE YOUR IDEAL SELF CARE ROUTINE AND HOW YOU WOULD LIKE IT TO IMPACT YOUR FUTURE

HOW WOULD I SPEAK TO MYSELF? (HINT: AS I WOULD SPEAK TO MY BEST FRIEND!)

WHAT HABITS WOULD BE FUN TO ADD TO MY DAILY ROUTINE?

HOW WOULD I PRESENT MY TRUE SELF TO THE WORLD?

HOW WOULD I INPSIRE OTHERS?

WHO/WHAT WILL SUPPORT ME ALONG THIS JOURNEY?

HOW WOULD I HANDLE TRIGGERING OR CHALLENGING SITUATIONS?

WHAT GOALS WOULD I LIKE ACCOMPLISH IN THE NEAR FUTURE?

vision board

ADD SOME IMAGES, QUOTES OR AFFIRMATIONS HERE THAT INSPIRE YOU AND REVIEW THEM DURING YOUR SELF CARE ROUTINE

vision board

vision board

people that inspire me

daily check-in

M T W T F S S

Date/Time:

○○○   ✕

How am I feeling?

Today I am looking forward to...

----

what am I grateful for today?

How can I add some fun to my day?

Today's affirmation:

Today's Mood

😆   🙂   😐   🙁   😣

Very Happy   Neutral   Very Sad

daily check-in

M T W T F S S

Date/Time:

○○○   ✕

How am I feeling?

Today I am looking forward to...

What am I grateful for today?

How can I add some fun to my day?

Today's affirmation:

Today's Mood

Very Happy   Neutral   Very Sad

daily check-in

M T W T F S S

Date/Time:

How am I feeling?

----

what am I grateful for today?

Today I am looking forward to...

How can I add some fun to my day?

Today's affirmation:

Today's Mood

Very Happy   Neutral   Very Sad

daily
check-in

M T W T F S S

Date/Time:

How am I feeling?

Today I am looking forward to...

What am I grateful for today?

How can I add some fun to my day?

Today's affirmation:

Today's Mood

Very Happy   Neutral   Very Sad

daily
check-in

M T W T F S S

Date/Time:

How am I feeling?

Today I am looking forward to...

----

what am I grateful for today?

How can I add some fun to my day?

Today's affirmation:

Today's Mood

Very Happy   Neutral   Very Sad

daily
check-in

M   T   W   T   F   S   S

Date/Time:

○○○   ✕

How am I feeling?

Today I am looking forward to...

What am I grateful for today?

How can I add some fun to my day?

Today's affirmation:

Today's Mood

😆   🙂   😐   🙁   😣

Very Happy   Neutral   Very Sad

daily check-in

M   T   W   T   F   S   S

Date/Time:

○○○   ✕

How am I feeling?

Today I am looking forward to...

----

what am I grateful for today?

How can I add some fun to my day?

Today's affirmation:

Today's Mood

😆 🙂 😐 🙁 😣

Very Happy   Neutral   Very Sad

daily
check-in

M T W T F S S

Date/Time:

How am I feeling?

Today I am looking forward to...

What am I grateful for today?

How can I add some fun to my day?

Today's affirmation:

Today's Mood

Very Happy   Neutral   Very Sad

daily
check-in

M T W T F S S

Date/Time:

How am I feeling?

Today I am looking forward to...

----

what am I grateful for today?

How can I add some fun to my day?

Today's affirmation:

Today's Mood

Very Happy   Neutral   Very Sad

daily
check-in

M T W T F S S

Date/Time:

How am I feeling?

Today I am looking forward to...

What am I grateful for today?

How can I add some fun to my day?

Today's affirmation:

Today's Mood

Very Happy   Neutral   Very Sad

daily check-in

M T W T F S S

Date/Time:

○○○   ✕

How am I feeling?

----

what am I grateful for today?

Today I am looking forward to...

How can I add some fun to my day?

Today's affirmation:

Today's Mood

😆   🙂   😐   🙁   😣

Very Happy   Neutral   Very Sad

daily check-in

M T W T F S S

Date/Time:

○○○   ✕

How am I feeling?

Today I am looking forward to...

What am I grateful for today?

How can I add some fun to my day?

Today's affirmation:

Today's Mood

😆 🙂 😐 🙁 😣

Very Happy   Neutral   Very Sad

daily
check-in

M T W T F S S

Date/Time:

○ ○ ○   ✕

How am I feeling?

Today I am looking forward to...

----

what am I grateful for today?

How can I add some fun to my day?

Today's affirmation:

Today's Mood

😆 🙂 😐 🙁 😣

Very Happy   Neutral   Very Sad

daily check-in

M T W T F S S

Date/Time:

How am I feeling?

Today I am looking forward to...

What am I grateful for today?

How can I add some fun to my day?

Today's affirmation:

Today's Mood

Very Happy   Neutral   Very Sad

daily
check-in

M T W T F S S

Date/Time:

How am I feeling?

Today I am looking forward to...

----

what am I grateful for today?

How can I add some fun to my day?

Today's affirmation:

Today's Mood

Very Happy   Neutral   Very Sad

daily check-in

M T W T F S S

Date/Time:

○○○   ✕

How am I feeling?

Today I am looking forward to...

What am I grateful for today?

How can I add some fun to my day?

Today's affirmation:

Today's Mood

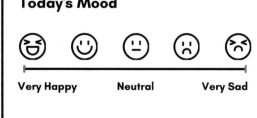

Very Happy   Neutral   Very Sad

daily
check-in

M T W T F S S

Date/Time:

○ ○ ○   ✕

How am I feeling?

Today I am looking forward to...

----

what am I grateful for today?

How can I add some fun to my day?

Today's affirmation:

Today's Mood

😆 🙂 😐 🙁 😫

Very Happy   Neutral   Very Sad

daily
check-in

M T W T F S S

Date/Time:

How am I feeling?

What am I grateful for today?

Today I am looking forward to...

How can I add some fun to my day?

Today's affirmation:

Today's Mood

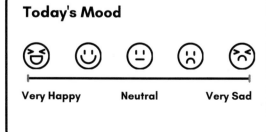

Very Happy   Neutral   Very Sad

daily
check-in

M T W T F S S

Date/Time:

How am I feeling?

Today I am looking forward to...

----

what am I grateful for today?

How can I add some fun to my day?

Today's affirmation:

Today's Mood

Very Happy   Neutral   Very Sad

daily check-in

M T W T F S S

Date/Time:

○ ○ ○   ✕

How am I feeling?

Today I am looking forward to...

What am I grateful for today?

How can I add some fun to my day?

Today's affirmation:

Today's Mood

😆 🙂 😐 🙁 😣

Very Happy   Neutral   Very Sad

gratitude

START YOUR DAY WITH GRATITUDE

I AM GRATEFUL FOR:

WHAT IS MAKING ME SMILE?

WHO/WHAT CAN I EMBRACE MORE IN MY DAILY LIFE?

GOOD THINGS THAT HAPPENED RECENTLY:

NOTES/DOODLES/REFLECTIONS:

self esteem boost

LET'S WORK ON BUILDING UP OUR CONFIDENCE AND SELF IMAGE

LIST MY WINS AND ACCOMPLISHEMENTS

A TIME I FELT CONFIDENT AND HOW I MANAGED IT

A MISTAKE AND HOW I TURNED IT INTO A POSITIVE

CREATE MY OWN AFFIRMATION ("I AM...", KEEP IT SHORT, PRESENT TENSE}

NOTES/DOODLES/REFLECTIONS:

worry journal

WORKING THROUGH ANYTHING THAT'S ON OUR MINDS BY EITHER LETTING GO
OR TAKING BACK CONTROL

A CURRENT WORRY:	SOMETHING I DO ABOUT IT?
A CURRENT WORRY:	SOMETHING I DO ABOUT IT?
A CURRENT WORRY:	SOMETHING I DO ABOUT IT?

worry journal

A CURRENT WORRY:

SOMETHING I DO ABOUT IT?

A CURRENT WORRY:

SOMETHING I DO ABOUT IT?

A CURRENT WORRY:

SOMETHING I DO ABOUT IT?

worry journal

A CURRENT WORRY:	SOMETHING I DO ABOUT IT?

A CURRENT WORRY:	SOMETHING I DO ABOUT IT?

A CURRENT WORRY:	SOMETHING I DO ABOUT IT?

worry journal

A CURRENT WORRY:

SOMETHING I DO ABOUT IT?

A CURRENT WORRY:

SOMETHING I DO ABOUT IT?

A CURRENT WORRY:

SOMETHING I DO ABOUT IT?

goals journal

LIST OUT AND MAKE AN ACTION PLAN FOR SOME IMPORTANT GOALS

SHORT TERM GOAL:

THINGS I CAN DO TO REACH MY GOAL:

SHORT TERM GOAL:

THINGS I CAN DO TO REACH MY GOAL:

SHORT TERM GOAL:

THINGS I CAN DO TO REACH MY GOAL:

goals journal

SHORT TERM GOAL:

THINGS I CAN DO TO REACH MY GOAL:

SHORT TERM GOAL:

THINGS I CAN DO TO REACH MY GOAL:

SHORT TERM GOAL:

THINGS I CAN DO TO REACH MY GOAL:

goals journal

SHORT TERM GOAL:	THINGS I CAN DO TO REACH MY GOAL:
SHORT TERM GOAL:	THINGS I CAN DO TO REACH MY GOAL:
SHORT TERM GOAL:	THINGS I CAN DO TO REACH MY GOAL:

goals journal

SHORT TERM GOAL:

THINGS I CAN DO TO REACH MY GOAL:

SHORT TERM GOAL:

THINGS I CAN DO TO REACH MY GOAL:

SHORT TERM GOAL:

THINGS I CAN DO TO REACH MY GOAL:

brain dump

TAKE A LOAD OFF AND LEAVE BEHIND OLD NEGATIVE THOUGHTS FOR GOOD,
WHILE BRAINSTORMING ANYTHING POSITIVE THAT COMES TO MIND!

FEARS

DISTRACTIONS

WORRIES

DISAPPOINTMENTS

SADNESS

INCOMPLETE GOALS

brain dump

ENCOURAGING THOUGHTS

FUN IDEAS

THINGS I'D LIKE TO DO SOMEDAY

PAST ACHIEVEMENTS

HAPPY MEMORIES

FUTURE GOALS

permission slip

USE THIS PAGE TO FIGURE OUT WHAT YOU WANT AND NEED TODAY FOR YOUR SELF CARE NEEDS, THEN GRANT YOURSELF THE PERMISSION TO TAKE IT!

TODAY I NEED:

TODAY I WANT:

TODAY I HAVE PERMISSION TO:

TODAY'S SELF CARE ACTIVITIES:

NOTES/DOODLES/REFLECTIONS:

cures for boredom

BAKE

WRITE TO SOMEONE

BE ACTIVE

PICK FLOWERS

WATCH A SUNSET

TAKE SOME PHOTOS

CALL A FRIEND

HAVE A PICNIC

AUDIOBOOK

my beautiful self

USE THE FOLLOWING DIAGRAMS (OR SKETCH OUT YOUR OWN IF YOU'D PREFER) TO SCRIBBLE, DOODLE AND WRITE POSITIVE WORDS AND COMPLIMENTS THAT REFLECT YOUR OWN BEAUTIFUL BODY, MIND AND SPIRIT!

my beautiful self

my beautiful self

my beautiful self

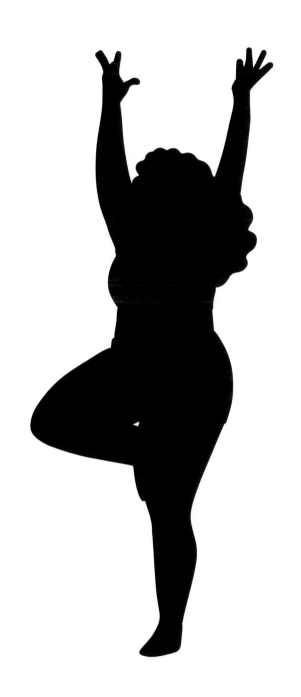

my beautiful self

my beautiful self

my beautiful self

my beautiful self

my support system

WE ALL NEED SOMEONE TO RELY ON IN DIFFICULT TIMES. USE THIS PAGE TO IDENTIFY THOSE PEOPLE AND EXPRESS GRATITUDE FOR THEM.

WHO CAN I CALL ON IN TIMES OF NEED?

WAYS IN WHICH THEY SUPPORT ME:

THEY ADD VALUE TO MY LIFE BY...

I ADD VALUE TO THEIR LIFE BY...

WHY I AM GRATEFUL FOR MY SUPPORT SYSTEM:

friendship goals

FRIENDSHIP ONE OF THE MOST VALUABLE AND IMPORTANT ASPECTS OF OUR YOUNG LIVES, BUT SOMETIMES COMPLICATED. LET'S ANALYSE WHAT FRIENDSHIP MEANS TO US.

QUALITIES OF A GOOD FRIEND:

QUALITIES OF A BAD FRIEND:

WAYS TO MAKE FRIENDS:

WHAT IS FRIENDSHIP TO ME?

BEST FRIENDSHIP ACTIVITIES:

FRIENDSHIP RULES:

planning my future

GET EXCITED ABOUT ALL THAT I HAVE TO LOOK FORWARD TO IN THE NEAR AND DISTANT FUTURE

WHERE WOULD I LIKE TO LIVE?

MY DREAM CAREER IS...

TRAVELS AND ADVENTURES:

MY DREAM RELATIONSHIPS (PARTNER/FAMILY/FRIENDS):

NOTES/DOODLES/REFLECTIONS:

about me

DISCOVERING MORE ABOUT MYSELF

MY FAVORITE MEMORY...

MY FAVORITE TOPIC...

I'M MOST HAPPY WHEN...

MY FAVORITE PERSON...

IF I HAD A MILLION DOLLARS I WOULD...

A FACT THAT MOST PEOPLE DON'T KNOW ABOUT ME...

about me

THE LAST THING I ATE...

THE LAST THING I WATCHED...

THE LAST PERSON I SPOKE TO...

TODAY, I FEEL...

DISCOVERIES/REFLECTIONS:

doodle challenge

DRAW A DOODLE FOR EACH TOPIC

THE INGREDIENTS OF MY FAVORITE DISH	MY BEST FRIEND
SOMETHING I CAN'T LIVE WITHOUT	**MY FAVORITE DRINK**
MY FAVORITE PATTERN	**SOMETHING I COLLECT**

doodle challenge

THE WORST HAIRCUT I EVER HAD	ONE PLACE I WANT TO VISIT
MY FAVORITE WORD	**MY PET**
MY FAVORITE OUTFIT	**MY FAVORITE FAST FOOD**

things that I can do for myself

LIST SOME FUN ACTIVITIES TO REFER BACK TO WHENEVER YOU FEEL THE NEED TO HAVE SOME MOOD-BOOSTING ME TIME AND SHOW YOURSELF SOME LOVE (FOR EXAMPLE: TREAT YOURSELF, TAKE A SELF CARE DAY, SPEND TIME IN NATURE, HAVE A DATE WITH A GOOD FRIEND, PAMPER YOURSELF, READ A BOOK, SPEND TIME ON A HOBBY).

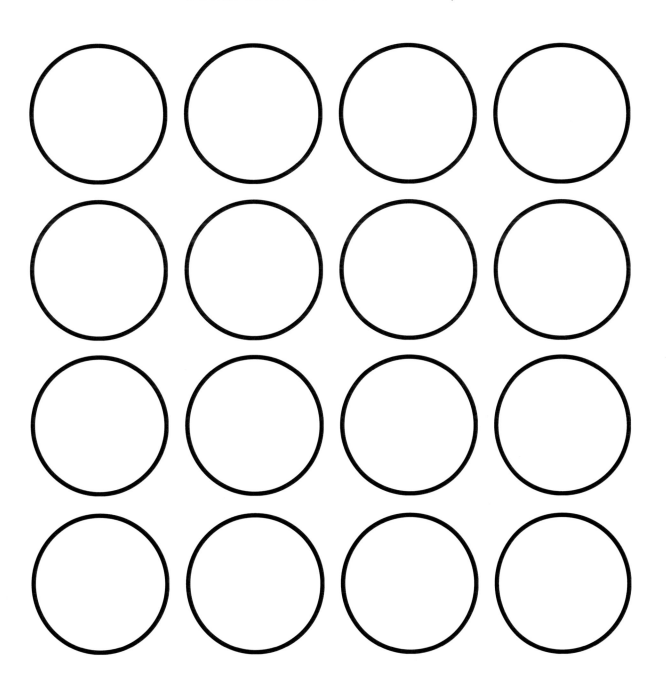

me from a-z

MAKE A LIST OF POSITIVE DESCRIBING WORDS THAT FIT ME, ONE WORD FROM A TO Z

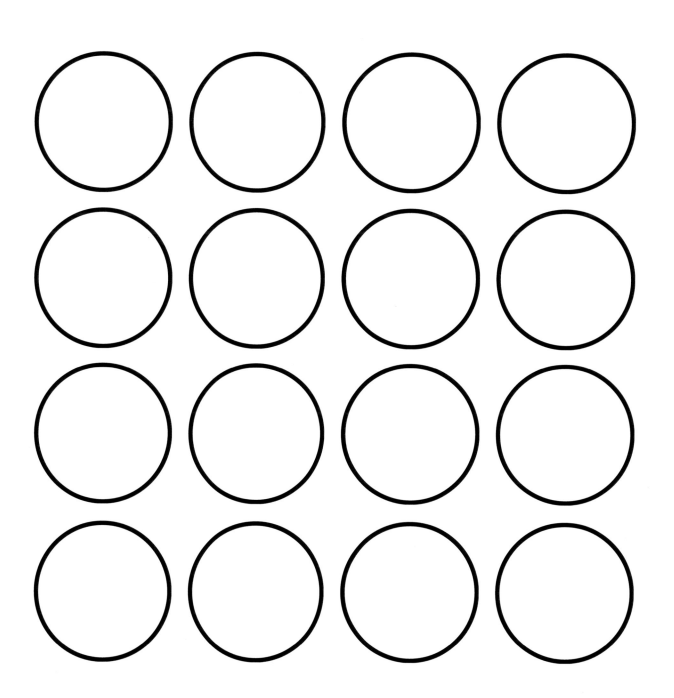

me from a-z

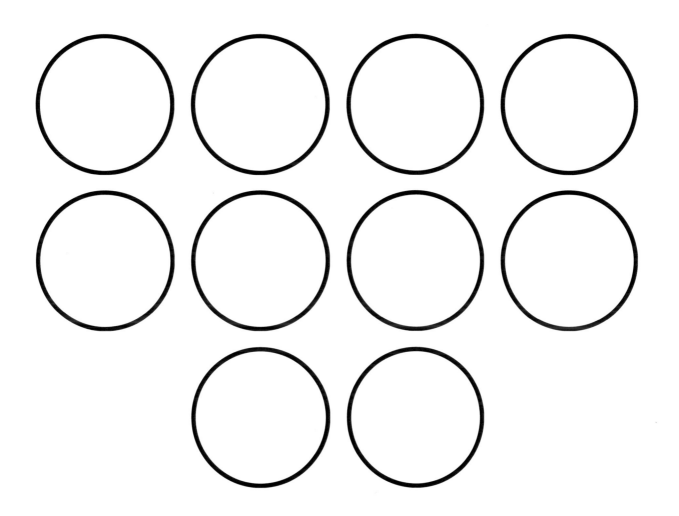

BONUS WORDS / DOODLES

today's mood

USE THIS PAGE TO:
- WRITE WORDS OR PHRASES THAT RESONATE WITH HOW YOU'RE FEELING TODAY,
- SKETCH OR DOODLE ANYTHING THAT DESCRIBES YOUR CURRENT STATE OF MIND,
- CURRENT WORLD EVENTS AND HOW THEY IMPACT MY MOOD,
- USE COLORS THAT REFLECT YOUR MOOD

today's mood

USE THIS PAGE TO:
- WRITE WORDS OR PHRASES THAT RESONATE WITH HOW YOU'RE FEELING TODAY,
- SKETCH OR DOODLE ANYTHING THAT DESCRIBES YOUR CURRENT STATE OF MIND,
- CURRENT WORLD EVENTS AND HOW THEY IMPACT MY MOOD,
- USE COLORS THAT REFLECT YOUR MOOD

today's mood

USE THIS PAGE TO:
- WRITE WORDS OR PHRASES THAT RESONATE WITH HOW YOU'RE FEELING TODAY,
- SKETCH OR DOODLE ANYTHING THAT DESCRIBES YOUR CURRENT STATE OF MIND,
- CURRENT WORLD EVENTS AND HOW THEY IMPACT MY MOOD,
- USE COLORS THAT REFLECT YOUR MOOD

today's mood

USE THIS PAGE TO:
- WRITE WORDS OR PHRASES THAT RESONATE WITH HOW YOU'RE FEELING TODAY,
- SKETCH OR DOODLE ANYTHING THAT DESCRIBES YOUR CURRENT STATE OF MIND,
- CURRENT WORLD EVENTS AND HOW THEY IMPACT MY MOOD,
- USE COLORS THAT REFLECT YOUR MOOD

today's mood

USE THIS PAGE TO:
- WRITE WORDS OR PHRASES THAT RESONATE WITH HOW YOU'RE FEELING TODAY,
- SKETCH OR DOODLE ANYTHING THAT DESCRIBES YOUR CURRENT STATE OF MIND,
- CURRENT WORLD EVENTS AND HOW THEY IMPACT MY MOOD,
- USE COLORS THAT REFLECT YOUR MOOD

today's mood

USE THIS PAGE TO:
- WRITE WORDS OR PHRASES THAT RESONATE WITH HOW YOU'RE FEELING TODAY,
- SKETCH OR DOODLE ANYTHING THAT DESCRIBES YOUR CURRENT STATE OF MIND,
- CURRENT WORLD EVENTS AND HOW THEY IMPACT MY MOOD,
- USE COLORS THAT REFLECT YOUR MOOD

today's mood

today's mood

USE THIS PAGE TO:
- WRITE WORDS OR PHRASES THAT RESONATE WITH HOW YOU'RE FEELING TODAY,
- SKETCH OR DOODLE ANYTHING THAT DESCRIBES YOUR CURRENT STATE OF MIND,
- CURRENT WORLD EVENTS AND HOW THEY IMPACT MY MOOD,
- USE COLORS THAT REFLECT YOUR MOOD

today's mood

USE THIS PAGE TO:
- WRITE WORDS OR PHRASES THAT RESONATE WITH HOW YOU'RE FEELING TODAY,
- SKETCH OR DOODLE ANYTHING THAT DESCRIBES YOUR CURRENT STATE OF MIND,
- CURRENT WORLD EVENTS AND HOW THEY IMPACT MY MOOD,
- USE COLORS THAT REFLECT YOUR MOOD

today's mood

USE THIS PAGE TO:
- WRITE WORDS OR PHRASES THAT RESONATE WITH HOW YOU'RE FEELING TODAY,
- SKETCH OR DOODLE ANYTHING THAT DESCRIBES YOUR CURRENT STATE OF MIND,
- CURRENT WORLD EVENTS AND HOW THEY IMPACT MY MOOD,
- USE COLORS THAT REFLECT YOUR MOOD

affirmations

- I AM PROUD OF MY PAST THAT HAS MADE ME WHO I AM
- MY FEELINGS ARE VALID
- I AM IN CHARGE OF MY LIFE
- I AM PROUD TO BE MYSELF
- I CAN MAKE MY DREAMS COME TRUE
- ANY PROBLEM I COME ACROSS HAS A SOLUTION
- MY TRUE SELF IS PERFECT
- I WILL BE PRESENT IN EVERY MOMENT
- I HAVE BELIEF IN MYSELF AND MY ABILITIES
- I'M DISCOVERING MY POWER
- I CAN STEP OUT OF MY COMFORT ZONE
- NO ONE CAN MAKE ME FEEL INFERIOR
- I CAN OVERCOME MY FEARS
- THE FUTURE IS BRIGHT FOR ME
- I HAVE SO MANY HAPPY DAYS AHEAD
- I AM WORTHY OF RESPECT
- EVERYTHING WILL BE OK
- I'VE DECIDED THAT I'M GOOD ENOUGH
- I HAVE COURAGE
- I AM ALLOWED TO FEEL CONFIDENT AND STAND OUT
- EVERY DAY IS A NEW BEGINNING
- I AM WORTHY OF MY BIGGEST DREAMS
- I AM DESERVING OF LOVE
- I AM READY TO LEARN
- I HAVE THE POWER TO CHANGE MY STORY
- MY STRENGTHS ARE GREATER THAN MY WEAKNESSES
- I AM STRONGER THAN I KNOW
- I WILL SHINE
- I AM RIGHT WHERE I'M SUPPOSED TO BE
- I WILL NOT APOLOGIZE FOR WHO I AM BECOMING
- I AM EQUIPPED WITH EVERYTHING I NEED
- MY OPINIONS COUNT
- I CAN DO HARD THINGS
- WHAT I THINK MATTERS
- I CAN DARE TO BE DIFFERENT
- I WILL NOT ALLOW ANYONE ELSE TO DICTATE WHO I WILL BE
- MY WELLBEING IS IMPORTANT
- I WILL NOT SHRINK WHO I AM
- I LOVE MYSELF
- I BELONG AS MUCH AS ANYONE ELSE
- I EMBRACE AND ADAPT TO CHANGE
- THE SAME GOOD I SEE IN OTHERS IS WITHIN ME TOO
- I LET GO OF ANY BELIEFS THAT HOLD ME BACK
- I MOVE THROUGH MY DAY WITH LOVE
- I WILL MAKE A DIFFERENCE
- I WILL NOT SPEND MY LIFE AT WAR WITH MYSELF
- I HAVE THE POWER TO MAKE CHANGE IN THE WORLD

quotes and affirmations

MAKE NOTE OF YOUR FAVORITE QUOTES TO REFER TO FOR A BOOST OF INSPIRATION.

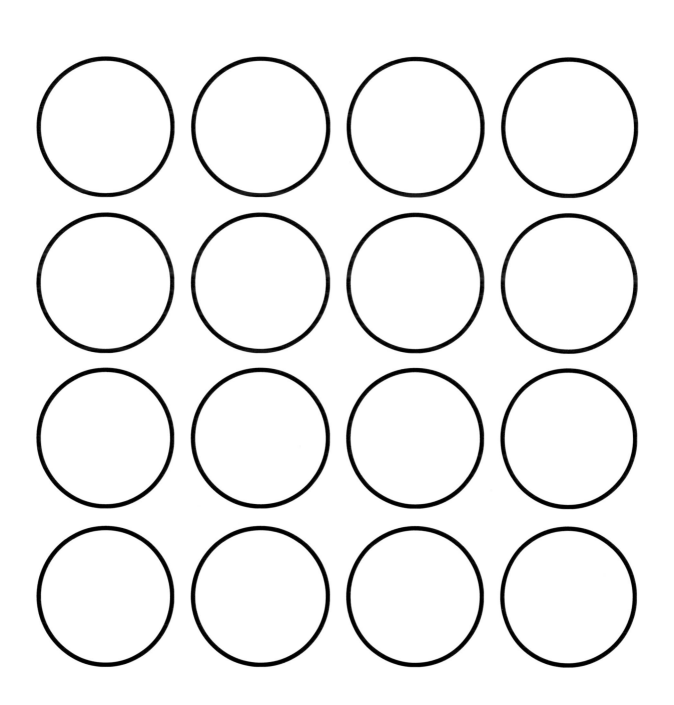

i have a bright future

i can be anything i want

i am valid

i have a voice

i am supported

i accept myself

good things are coming

i can face challenges

social media analysis

HOW DOES MY CURRENT SOCIAL MEDIA CONSUMPTION MAKE ME FEEL?

HOW WOULD I LIKE TO FEEL AFTER SPENDING TIME ON SOCIAL MEDIA?

WHAT CHANGES CAN I MAKE TO BRIDGE THAT GAP (LIMIT TIME ON SOCIAL MEDIA, UNFOLLOW CONTENT THAT DOESN'T SERVE ME)?

social media analysis

WHAT ARE SOME ACTIVITIES I CAN DO TO REPLACE TIME SPENT ONLINE WHEN IT DOES NOT SERVE ME?

ARE THERE WAYS THAT I CAN USE SOCIAL MEDIA TO IMPROVE MY SELF IMAGE (SOME IDEAS: FOLLOW INSPIRING PEOPLE OF MY AGE, CREATE MY OWN CONTENT, CONNECT WITH POSITIVE INFLUENCES)?

WRITE SOME FACTS AND REMINDERS HERE TO REFER TO WHEN EXPERIENCING NEGATIVE THOUGHTS AFTER SPENDING TIME ON SOCIAL MEDIA

screen time tracker

DATE	TV/MOVIE	PHONE/TABLET	GAMING	TOTAL

screen time tracker

DATE	TV/MOVIE	PHONE/TABLET	GAMING	TOTAL

screen time tracker

DATE	TV/MOVIE	PHONE/TABLET	GAMING	TOTAL

screen time tracker

DATE	TV/MOVIE	PHONE/TABLET	GAMING	TOTAL

sleep tracker

DATE	BED TIME	WAKE TIME	TOTAL HOURS	QUALITY (OUT OF 10)

sleep tracker

DATE	BED TIME	WAKE TIME	TOTAL HOURS	QUALITY (OUT OF 10)

sleep tracker

DATE	BED TIME	WAKE TIME	TOTAL HOURS	QUALITY (OUT OF 10)

sleep tracker

DATE	BED TIME	WAKE TIME	TOTAL HOURS	QUALITY (OUT OF 10)

self care challenge

day 1
WATCH THE SUNRISE

day 2
VISIT A MARKET

day 3
HYDRATE!

day 4
GET DRESSED UP

day 5
START A NEW HABIT

day 6
DANCE!

day 7
PAMPER YOURSELF

day 8
COMPLIMENT YOURSELF

day 9
SPEND TIME WITH FAMILY

day 10
GIVE BACK TO YOUR COMMUNITY

day 11
20 MINUTE MEDITATION

day 12
TRY A FUN WORKOUT

day 13
LISTEN TO YOUR FAVE PLAYLIST

day 14
PRACTICE GRATITUDE

day 15
DO SOMETHING OUTSIDE

day 16
TAKE LOTS OF PHOTOS

self care challenge

day 17

START A NEW BOOK

day 18

SOCIAL MEDIA UNFOLLOW SPREE

day 19

MAKE A GOAL FOR THIS MONTH

day 20

MAKE A VISION BOARD

day 21

PLAN A FRIEND DATE

day 22

FIND A NEW CREATIVE HOBBY

day 23

FIND A CAUSE TO SUPPORT

day 24

JOURNAL FOR SELF DISCOVERY

day 25

ORGANISE MY SPACE

day 26

TAKE A RELAXING BATH

day 27

SET A NEW LIFE GOAL

day 28

SOCIAL MEDIA DETOX DAY

day 29

SIGN PETITIONS THAT I STAND WITH

day 30

GO FOR A MINDFUL WALK

my playlist

SONGS THAT INSPIRE AND UPLIFT ME RIGHT NOW

ARTIST	SONG

reading list

BOOKS THAT I'D LIKE TO READ IN THE NEAR FUTURE

TITLE	AUTHOR

to watch list

MOVIES AND SHOWS THAT I'M DYING TO WATCH

MOVIE

SHOW

----

fun activities

IDEAS FOR FUN ACTIVITIES TO MAKE MEMORIES

PLACE/PERSON	ACTIVITY
--------------------------------	--------------------------------
--------------------------------	--------------------------------
--------------------------------	--------------------------------
--------------------------------	--------------------------------
--------------------------------	--------------------------------
--------------------------------	--------------------------------
--------------------------------	--------------------------------
--------------------------------	--------------------------------
--------------------------------	--------------------------------
--------------------------------	--------------------------------
--------------------------------	--------------------------------
--------------------------------	--------------------------------
--------------------------------	--------------------------------
--------------------------------	--------------------------------
--------------------------------	--------------------------------
--------------------------------	--------------------------------
--------------------------------	--------------------------------

recipes

FUN RECIPES I'VE DISCOVERED AND WOULD LIKE TO TRY

seasonal loves

MY FAVORITE THINGS AND ACTIVITIES ABOUT EACH SEASON

SPRING

SUMMER

----

seasonal loves

MY FAVORITE THINGS AND ACTIVITIES ABOUT EACH SEASON

FALL

WINTER

----

journal

TAKE SOME TIME TO CLEAR YOUR MIND AND PUT YOUR THOUGHTS TO PAPER.
LET IT FLOW NATURALLY OR USE ONE OF OUR SAMPLE PROMPTS:

- WHAT WOULD I SAY TO MY YOUNGER SELF?
- WHAT WOULD I SAY TO MY FUTURE SELF?
- IF I COULD MEET SOMEONE WHO INSPIRES ME WHO WOULD IT BE?
- WHAT AM I MOST LOOKING FORWARD TO IN THE FUTURE?
- PEOPLE I AM GRATEFUL FOR
- HOW WOULD MY BEST FRIEND DESCRIBE ME?
- HOW CAN I GIVE BACK?
- I FEEL MOST ALIVE WHEN...
- MY FAVORITE SONG AND WHY
- WHERE DO I SEE MYSELF A YEAR FROM NOW?
- MY FAVORITE DAY OF THE WEEK AND WHY
- MY BIGGEST ACCOMPLISHMENT IN LIFE SO FAR
- WHAT I MISS (OR WILL MISS) MOST ABOUT SCHOOL
- MY SUPERPOWER IS...
- ONE THING THAT IS WORRYING ME CURRENTLY AND WHY
- AN OBSTACLE THAT I'VE OVERCOME
- 5 THINGS I ADMIRE ABOUT MYSELF
- THE BEST COMPLIMENT I'VE RECEIVED AND HOW IT MADE ME FEEL
- IF I COULD SWAP LIVES WITH ONE PERSON FOR ONE DAY WHO WOULD IT BE AND WHY?
- THE BEST TRIP I'VE EVER TAKEN
- SOMETHING I'M LOOKING FORWARD TO IN THE NEAR FUTURE
- MY THREE BIGGEST GOALS CURRENTLY
- HOW DO I RELEASE STRESS?
- WHAT AM I PROCRASTINATING ON AT THE MOMENT? WHY?
- THE BEST THING ABOUT BEING MY AGE IS...
- WHO WOULD I LOVE TO MEET AND WHY?
- HOW WOULD I DESCRIBE MYSELF TO SOMEONE I'VE NEVER MET?
- WHAT EXCITES ME MOST ABOUT THE FUTURE?
- SOMETHING SMALL THAT MAKES ME HAPPY
- I FEEL MOST CONFIDENT WHEN...
- A HOBBY THAT BRINGS ME JOY
- THE MOST PRECIOUS THING I OWN
- MY FAVORITE SUMMER MEMORY
- HOW DO I DEFINE SUCCESS?
- HOW COMFORTABLE AM I IN VOICING MY FEELINGS?
- WHAT ARE MY STRENGTHS AND WEAKNESSES?
- WRITE A LETTER TO SOMEONE, ANYONE
- WHAT DO I SEE WHEN I LOOK IN THE MIRROR?
- HOW DO I WANT TO BE FOR MYSELF AND OTHERS TODAY?
- WHAT IS A LESSON THAT I'VE LEARNED RECENTLY?
- ONE MEMORY I'D LIKE TO RELIVE
- DESCRIBE MY PERFECT DAY
- SOMEONE OR SOMETHING I CAN'T LIVE WITHOUT
- IF/WHEN I BECOME A PARENT, WHAT KIND OF PARENT WILL I BE?
- THE BEST PIECE OF ADVICE I'VE RECEIVED
- THE HIGHLIGHT OF TODAY WAS...

journal

journal

journal

journal

journal

journal

journal

journal

journal

journal

habit tracker

GENTLY BUILD HABITS THAT SERVE YOU AND IMPROVE YOUR SELF IMAGE.
(FOR EXAMPLE: LIMIT TIME SPENT ON SOCIAL MEDIA, MEDITATE, PRACTICE
GRATITUDE, USE THIS WORKBOOK, JOURNAL, PRACTICE SELF CARE AND
POSITIVE SELF TALK).
WE'VE INCLUDED DIFFERENT FORMATS AND PLENTY OF SPACE FOR THIS
IMPORTANT EXERCISE.

START DATE: 1st March   END DATE: 30th March

HABIT: track my sleep cycle

X	X	X	4	5	6	7
8	9	10	11	12	13	14
15	16	17	18	19	20	21
22	23	24	25	26	27	28
29	30	31	32	33	34	35
36	37	38	39	40	41	42
43	44	45	46	47	48	49

EXAMPLE

REASONS: wake up feeling more rested, have more of a routine

START DATE: END DATE:

HABIT:

1	2	3	4	5
6	7	8	9	10
11	12	13	14	15
16	17	18	19	20
21	22	23	24	25
26	27	28	29	30

REASONS:

START DATE: _____   END DATE: _____

HABIT: _____

1	2	3	4	5
6	7	8	9	10
11	12	13	14	15
16	17	18	19	20
21	22	23	24	25
26	27	28	29	30

REASONS: _____

START DATE: END DATE:

HABIT:

1	2	3	4	5
6	7	8	9	10
11	12	13	14	15
16	17	18	19	20
21	22	23	24	25
26	27	28	29	30

REASONS:

START DATE: END DATE:

HABIT:

1	2	3	4	5
6	7	8	9	10
11	12	13	14	15
16	17	18	19	20
21	22	23	24	25
26	27	28	29	30

REASONS:

START DATE: END DATE:

HABIT:

1	2	3	4	5
6	7	8	9	10
11	12	13	14	15
16	17	18	19	20
21	22	23	24	25
26	27	28	29	30

REASONS:

START DATE: _____   END DATE: _____

HABIT: _____

1	2	3	4	5
6	7	8	9	10
11	12	13	14	15
16	17	18	19	20
21	22	23	24	25
26	27	28	29	30

REASONS:

START DATE: _____ END DATE: _____

HABIT: _____

1	2	3	4	5
6	7	8	9	10
11	12	13	14	15
16	17	18	19	20
21	22	23	24	25
26	27	28	29	30

REASONS:

START DATE: [   ]   END DATE: [   ]

HABIT: [   ]

1	2	3	4	5
6	7	8	9	10
11	12	13	14	15
16	17	18	19	20
21	22	23	24	25
26	27	28	29	30

REASONS:

START DATE: _____ END DATE: _____

HABIT: _____

1	2	3	4	5
6	7	8	9	10
11	12	13	14	15
16	17	18	19	20
21	22	23	24	25
26	27	28	29	30

REASONS:

HABIT:

1	2	3	4	5
6	7	8	9	10
11	12	13	14	15
16	17	18	19	20
21	22	23	24	25
26	27	28	29	30

HABIT:

1	2	3	4	5
6	7	8	9	10
11	12	13	14	15
16	17	18	19	20
21	22	23	24	25
26	27	28	29	30

HABIT:

1	2	3	4	5
6	7	8	9	10
11	12	13	14	15
16	17	18	19	20
21	22	23	24	25
26	27	28	29	30

HABIT:

1	2	3	4	5
6	7	8	9	10
11	12	13	14	15
16	17	18	19	20
21	22	23	24	25
26	27	28	29	30

HABIT:

1	2	3	4	5
6	7	8	9	10
11	12	13	14	15
16	17	18	19	20
21	22	23	24	25
26	27	28	29	30

HABIT:

1	2	3	4	5
6	7	8	9	10
11	12	13	14	15
16	17	18	19	20
21	22	23	24	25
26	27	28	29	30

HABIT:

1	2	3	4	5
6	7	8	9	10
11	12	13	14	15
16	17	18	19	20
21	22	23	24	25
26	27	28	29	30

HABIT:

1	2	3	4	5
6	7	8	9	10
11	12	13	14	15
16	17	18	19	20
21	22	23	24	25
26	27	28	29	30

HABIT:

1	2	3	4	5
6	7	8	9	10
11	12	13	14	15
16	17	18	19	20
21	22	23	24	25
26	27	28	29	30

HABIT:

1	2	3	4	5
6	7	8	9	10
11	12	13	14	15
16	17	18	19	20
21	22	23	24	25
26	27	28	29	30

HABIT:

1	2	3	4	5
6	7	8	9	10
11	12	13	14	15
16	17	18	19	20
21	22	23	24	25
26	27	28	29	30

HABIT:

1	2	3	4	5
6	7	8	9	10
11	12	13	14	15
16	17	18	19	20
21	22	23	24	25
26	27	28	29	30

HABIT:

1	2	3	4	5
6	7	8	9	10
11	12	13	14	15
16	17	18	19	20
21	22	23	24	25
26	27	28	29	30

HABIT:

1	2	3	4	5
6	7	8	9	10
11	12	13	14	15
16	17	18	19	20
21	22	23	24	25
26	27	28	29	30

HABIT:

1	2	3	4	5
6	7	8	9	10
11	12	13	14	15
16	17	18	19	20
21	22	23	24	25
26	27	28	29	30

HABIT:

1	2	3	4	5
6	7	8	9	10
11	12	13	14	15
16	17	18	19	20
21	22	23	24	25
26	27	28	29	30

HABIT:

1	2	3	4	5
6	7	8	9	10
11	12	13	14	15
16	17	18	19	20
21	22	23	24	25
26	27	28	29	30

HABIT:

1	2	3	4	5
6	7	8	9	10
11	12	13	14	15
16	17	18	19	20
21	22	23	24	25
26	27	28	29	30

HABIT:	1	2	3	4	5
	6	7	8	9	10
	11	12	13	14	15
	16	17	18	19	20
	21	22	23	24	25
	26	27	28	29	30

HABIT:	1	2	3	4	5
	6	7	8	9	10
	11	12	13	14	15
	16	17	18	19	20
	21	22	23	24	25
	26	27	28	29	30

HABIT:	1	2	3	4	5
	6	7	8	9	10
	11	12	13	14	15
	16	17	18	19	20
	21	22	23	24	25
	26	27	28	29	30

HABIT:	1	2	3	4	5
	6	7	8	9	10
	11	12	13	14	15
	16	17	18	19	20
	21	22	23	24	25
	26	27	28	29	30

HABIT:	1	2	3	4	5
	6	7	8	9	10
	11	12	13	14	15
	16	17	18	19	20
	21	22	23	24	25
	26	27	28	29	30

HABIT:	1	2	3	4	5
	6	7	8	9	10
	11	12	13	14	15
	16	17	18	19	20
	21	22	23	24	25
	26	27	28	29	30

HABIT:

1	2	3	4	5
6	7	8	9	10
11	12	13	14	15
16	17	18	19	20
21	22	23	24	25
26	27	28	29	30

HABIT:

1	2	3	4	5
6	7	8	9	10
11	12	13	14	15
16	17	18	19	20
21	22	23	24	25
26	27	28	29	30

HABIT:

1	2	3	4	5
6	7	8	9	10
11	12	13	14	15
16	17	18	19	20
21	22	23	24	25
26	27	28	29	30

HABIT:

1	2	3	4	5
6	7	8	9	10
11	12	13	14	15
16	17	18	19	20
21	22	23	24	25
26	27	28	29	30

HABIT:

1	2	3	4	5
6	7	8	9	10
11	12	13	14	15
16	17	18	19	20
21	22	23	24	25
26	27	28	29	30

HABIT:

1	2	3	4	5
6	7	8	9	10
11	12	13	14	15
16	17	18	19	20
21	22	23	24	25
26	27	28	29	30

HABIT:

1	2	3	4	5
6	7	8	9	10
11	12	13	14	15
16	17	18	19	20
21	22	23	24	25
26	27	28	29	30

HABIT:

1	2	3	4	5
6	7	8	9	10
11	12	13	14	15
16	17	18	19	20
21	22	23	24	25
26	27	28	29	30

HABIT:

1	2	3	4	5
6	7	8	9	10
11	12	13	14	15
16	17	18	19	20
21	22	23	24	25
26	27	28	29	30

HABIT:

1	2	3	4	5
6	7	8	9	10
11	12	13	14	15
16	17	18	19	20
21	22	23	24	25
26	27	28	29	30

HABIT:

1	2	3	4	5
6	7	8	9	10
11	12	13	14	15
16	17	18	19	20
21	22	23	24	25
26	27	28	29	30

HABIT:

1	2	3	4	5
6	7	8	9	10
11	12	13	14	15
16	17	18	19	20
21	22	23	24	25
26	27	28	29	30

HABIT:

1	2	3	4	5
6	7	8	9	10
11	12	13	14	15
16	17	18	19	20
21	22	23	24	25
26	27	28	29	30

HABIT:

1	2	3	4	5
6	7	8	9	10
11	12	13	14	15
16	17	18	19	20
21	22	23	24	25
26	27	28	29	30

HABIT:

1	2	3	4	5
6	7	8	9	10
11	12	13	14	15
16	17	18	19	20
21	22	23	24	25
26	27	28	29	30

HABIT:

1	2	3	4	5
6	7	8	9	10
11	12	13	14	15
16	17	18	19	20
21	22	23	24	25
26	27	28	29	30

HABIT:

1	2	3	4	5
6	7	8	9	10
11	12	13	14	15
16	17	18	19	20
21	22	23	24	25
26	27	28	29	30

HABIT:

1	2	3	4	5
6	7	8	9	10
11	12	13	14	15
16	17	18	19	20
21	22	23	24	25
26	27	28	29	30

1	2	3	4	5
6	7	8	9	10
11	12	13	14	15
16	17	18	19	20
21	22	23	24	25
26	27	28	29	30

1	2	3	4	5
6	7	8	9	10
11	12	13	14	15
16	17	18	19	20
21	22	23	24	25
26	27	28	29	30

1	2	3	4	5
6	7	8	9	10
11	12	13	14	15
16	17	18	19	20
21	22	23	24	25
26	27	28	29	30

1	2	3	4	5
6	7	8	9	10
11	12	13	14	15
16	17	18	19	20
21	22	23	24	25
26	27	28	29	30

1	2	3	4	5
6	7	8	9	10
11	12	13	14	15
16	17	18	19	20
21	22	23	24	25
26	27	28	29	30

1	2	3	4	5
6	7	8	9	10
11	12	13	14	15
16	17	18	19	20
21	22	23	24	25
26	27	28	29	30

HABIT:

1	2	3	4	5
6	7	8	9	10
11	12	13	14	15
16	17	18	19	20
21	22	23	24	25
26	27	28	29	30

HABIT:

1	2	3	4	5
6	7	8	9	10
11	12	13	14	15
16	17	18	19	20
21	22	23	24	25
26	27	28	29	30

HABIT:

1	2	3	4	5
6	7	8	9	10
11	12	13	14	15
16	17	18	19	20
21	22	23	24	25
26	27	28	29	30

HABIT:

1	2	3	4	5
6	7	8	9	10
11	12	13	14	15
16	17	18	19	20
21	22	23	24	25
26	27	28	29	30

HABIT:

1	2	3	4	5
6	7	8	9	10
11	12	13	14	15
16	17	18	19	20
21	22	23	24	25
26	27	28	29	30

HABIT:

1	2	3	4	5
6	7	8	9	10
11	12	13	14	15
16	17	18	19	20
21	22	23	24	25
26	27	28	29	30

love letter to myself

WITH LOVE AND COMPASSION, WRITE A LETTER TO YOURSELF.
RECOGNISE ANY CHALLENGES YOU HAVE OVERCOME AND ARE STILL FACING,
YOUR MANY STRENGTHS, WHAT YOU NOW ACCEPT ABOUT YOURSELF, WHAT
YOU NOW LOVE ABOUT YOURSELF AND WHO YOU ARE BECOMING, HOW YOU
WILL ADJUST FROM NOW ONWARDS

dear future me...

LOOK INTO YOUR BRIGHT FUTURE AND WRITE A LETTER TO LOOK BACK ON. DESCRIBE WHAT YOUR LIFE CURRENTLY LOOKS LIKE, YOUR DAILY ACTIVITIES, THE PEOPLE AROUND YOU, YOUR GOALS, STRUGGLES AND WHAT'S MOST IMPORTANT TO YOU RIGHT NOW.

to my favorite person

WRITE A LETTER TO THE PERSON THAT MEANS THE MOST TO YOU (FRIEND, FAMILY MEMBER, MENTOR). EXPRESS ANYTHING THAT IS IN YOUR HEART FROM YOUR FEELINGS OF GRATITUDE AND LOVE OR EXPLORE YOUR FUTURE ADVENTURES TOGETHER

reflections

WHAT NEW SELF CARE HABITS HAVE MADE THE BIGGEST DIFFERENCE IN HOW I FEEL ABOUT MYSELF?

WHAT HAS BEEN MY BIGGEST REALIZATION?

HAVE I COME TO REALIZE HOW SPECIAL I AM AND HOW BRIGHT MY FUTURE IS?

reflections

WHAT DO I LOVE ABOUT MYSELF?

WHAT IS MY ONE BIGGEST TAKE AWAY FROM THIS EXPERIENCE?

HOW WOULD I LIKE TO MOVE FORWARD ON MY SELF CARE JOURNEY?

notes

notes

notes

notes

notes

notes

notes

notes

notes

notes